RETURNING HOME

T0029342

Returning Home

the poetry of
Tao Yuan-ming

Translated by

Dan Veach

WHITE PINE PRESS | BUFFALO, NEW YORK

White Pine Press
P.O. Box 236
Buffalo, NY 14201
www.whitepine.org

Publication of this book was supported by the Witter Bynner Foundation for Poetry and by public funds from the New York State Council on the Arts, with the support of Governor Kathy Hochul and the New York State Legislature, a State Agency.

Acknowledgements: These poems previously appeared in:
Chrysanthemums: "Autumn Chrysanthemums," "Mr. Five Willows,"
        "Meeting with Fire," "Scolding My Sons"
Diode: "Moving House," "Begging for Food"
Kyoto Journal: "Returning to Fields and Gardens," "Reply to Secretary Kuo"
Notre Dame Review: "Elegy for Myself"
Terrene: "The Peach Blossom Spring"
Tupelo Quarterly: "The Bitter Cold Year," "Spring at My Farm, Think-
        ing of the Ancients," "Reading *The Classic of Mountains and Seas,*"
        "Enjoying Ourselves Under the Cypresses"

Cover Image: Shitao (1642–1707), Qing Dynasty (1644–1911) "Poetic Feeling of Tao Yuiangming." Palace Museum, Beijing, China.

Printed and bound in the United States of America.

ISBN 978-1-945680-69-4

Library of Congress Control Number: 2022950770

RETURNING HOME

Contents

INTRODUCTION

For the myriad shades that weave about this place
How can we thank Master Tao enough?
— Pei Ti, "Willow Waves"

Pei Ti's grateful reference to Tao Yuan-ming would be echoed by generations of Chinese poets, for whom Tao Yuan-ming was a beloved grandfather figure. Just as the Impressionists taught us to see in a new way, Tao taught the Chinese poets a lyrical attitude toward life. Pei Ti, enjoying the reflection of willows on the water, is reminded of "Mr. Five Willows," Tao's literary persona, and feels grateful to see these willows as a poet sees them, grateful to be a grandson of Tao.

Tao Yuan-ming, who lived around 400 A.D., stands first in the line of China's great lyric poets. Creator of an intimate, honest, plain-spoken style, Tao was a man whose life spoke as eloquently as his art. Indeed, no poet's life and art have ever been more of a piece.

The only major Chinese poet before him, Chu Yuan, was a high official who committed suicide in despair over the corruption of his dynasty. Tao, also born into corrupt and turbulent times, would commit a sort of "official suicide," quitting his post as Magistrate and retiring to live the humble and difficult life of a farmer.

He and his family would pay dearly for this choice, enduring hunger, cold and poverty. But he never wavered from it, holding steadfastly to the Confucian virtue of "firmness in adversity." For a scholar to live this kind of reclusive life, giving up wealth and power, represented the highest moral virtue to the Chinese. Indeed, in the history of his dynasty Tao is included not with the poets but with the recluses.

There is logic in this, for Tao's poetry flows directly from the choice to follow his own nature rather than the dictates of society. His best-known poem, "Returning Home," begins with the moment he makes that choice. From that day forward, his poems are a record of this conscious experiment in living. From the desolation of "The Bitter Cold Year" to the elation of "Reading *The Classic of Mountains and Seas,*" Tao shares his life freely and fully with us. Joy and suffering, pride and shame, nothing is held back. This had never been done before in Chinese poetry, and indeed it has hardly been equaled since.

Tao was given the posthumous title "Summoned Scholar of Tranquil Integrity." Integrity is certainly the first word that springs to mind in thinking of Tao. Tranquility is part of his popular image too: he is often depicted sniffing chrysanthemum blossoms and sipping wine. Some would say he worked hard to create this carefree image of himself—best summed up in his tongue-in-cheek self-portrait, "Mr. Five Willows." But his poetry, which brings us closer to him than his closest friends, takes us beneath this calm surface. Here we see that Tao's tranquility was the outcome of struggle and doubt, something hard-won, something worth celebrating. "Friends of Tao" more than a thousand years removed, we are fortunate to join in this celebration of a life well and truly lived.

The Life of Tao Yuan-ming

The most reliable biography of Tao Yuan-ming comes from his own writing and the funeral elegy by his friend Yen Yen-chih. He was regarded as important enough to appear in three dynastic histories, the first about fifty years after his death. These include some droll stories which, true or not, have since become part of Chinese folklore.

"May you live in interesting times"

Tao Yuan-ming lived from 365 to 427 A.D., a time that certainly fell under the ancient Chinese curse cited above. He was born in the Chin dynasty, during the turbulent Six Dynasties period (222-589) between the fall of the Han dynasty and the rise of the Tang. The Chin emperors had been driven out of north China by barbarian tribes, founding a new capital in the south near modern Nanjing. It was a period of chaotic struggle for power, much like the latter days of the Roman empire. Reason enough for a wise man to stay out of politics, even if he were not, like Tao, by nature averse to public life.

His great-grandfather Tao Kan had been Grand Marshal of the Chin, his grandfather a Prefect of Wuch'ang. His father was also an official, but the family seems to have come down in the world, as Tao frequently speaks of being raised in poverty. The wage of the lowest official was no more than a farmer would make. But it was a genteel poverty, enlightened by music and literature, the "lute and books" of which Tao was always so fond.

He came of age at twenty with the traditional capping ceremony. His first wife died soon after they set up house together. His second wife gave him several sons, but seems to have been (understandably) put out with him on occasion. The biographical sketch in Tao's collected works says that his wife endured toil quietly and shared his ideals. She must have endured much indeed, but not, if we can believe her husband, always quietly.

THE RELUCTANT MAGISTRATE

Like any good Confucian scholar, Tao entered government service. But he was unhappy as an official, resigning from his job as Provincial Libationer and refusing another post as Registrar. The name "Libationer" suggests involvement with official rituals. Surely pouring libations would not be a problem for someone as fond of wine as Tao. But this office was also typically in charge of the civil service examinations. Bribery and pressure to favor the wealthy and powerful came with the territory, and would have put our morally upright scholar in an impossible position.

Poverty forced him back into service, however, as traveling secretary to the general of the "Stabilization Army" and the "Establishing Majesty General" (both names suggesting a throne in peril). Here he had a front row seat on the political crises of his time. The weak Chin emperor[1] became the puppet of one powerful warlord after another. Civil conflict and popular rebellion continued until the overthrow of the dynasty by Liu Yu.

After arduous travels "over a thousand li" he finally got a job closer to home, as Magistrate of the little town of P'eng-tse. The dynastic histories record some P'eng-tse stories the Chinese have treasured ever since. They claim that Tao took the job because the public lands would grow enough rice to keep him in wine. He did not take his family with him, so he sent them a servant, accompanied by this note: "I am sending you this servant to help with the work of gathering wood and drawing water. He too is someone's son, and should be treated kindly." How a person behaves when given power is a great test of character. Tao seems to have passed the test.

But it was not in his nature to be a team player. When an Inspector visited P'eng-tse, Tao was advised to dress up and pay him a formal courtesy call. Tao gave a sigh and said, "For five pecks of rice I cannot kowtow to some village idiot." That same day he gave up his seal[2] and left his post. Tao gives a different account of his departure in the introduction to "Returning Home." But the result was the same: he would never hold office again.

POETRY VS POWER

His reputation as a recluse poet soon began to spread. The governor of his province, Wang Hung, was eager to visit him, but Tao (perhaps afraid of being offered a job) kept pleading illness. Finally Wang ordered one of Tao's friends to invite him to a wine party. After the two friends had been drinking for a while, Wang casually showed up. Tao was too far gone to object. Wang would prove to be a friend in need, sometimes providing Tao with food and even shoes when he found him barefoot.

The next governor, Tan Tao-chi, posed more of a

challenge. Tao was weak from hunger when Tan paid a visit. Tan asked him why he would not take office, citing the classic Confucian argument: "If the empire does not abide by the Way, a wise man will retire. But if it follows the Way, he comes forward to serve. You were born in an enlightened age—why do you make yourself suffer like this?"

It was a no-win situation. How could he tell the governor that the empire was not following the Way? Tan was, after all, his guest. Tao took the only way out, politely blaming himself: "How would I dare to be thought wise? I have no such ambition." Tan presented him with meat and grain, but Tao, not wanting to be in his debt, waved them away. Altogether an embarrassing episode. Little wonder Tao avoided those in power.

The dynastic histories speculate that, since Tao's great-grandfather had been Marshal of the Chin, Tao loyally refused to serve under the warlord Liu Yu, who first made puppets of the Chin emperors and then usurped the throne. Tao's last recorded refusal, of the position of Archivist, did occur around the time that Liu strangled Emperor An and overthrew the Chin dynasty. But Tao simply pleads illness (to his rulers) and lack of inclination (to his readers). If he had openly opposed Liu Yu, Tao's poetic career might have been "strangled" as well.

BEYOND BELIEF

Tao gave little credence to religious dogma, be it China's native Taoism or that exotic import from India, Buddhism. The histories record that when the Buddhist Master Hui-yuan was forming the Lotus Society, he invited Tao to be a member. Tao replied that he would join if he were allowed (very much against Buddhist rules) to drink wine. Hui-yuan was willing to make an exception and, according to Buddhist sources, Tao became a frequent visitor. This liberal attitude was typical of China, where Taoism, Buddhism and Confucianism mingled and borrowed freely from one another. All three came to use the term Tao (the Way) for both the ultimate Reality and the proper path for humanity to follow.

The Buddhists have another story about Tao Yuanming. Master Hui-yuan had vowed never to cross a little stream that marked the boundary of his Buddhist monastery. One day he was seeing off Tao Yuanming (a Confucian) and Lu Hsiu-ching (a Taoist). Absorbed in talking about the unity of the Tao, the three friends unwittingly crossed the little stream. As soon as they did so, a tiger roared. Seeing their friendship had caused Master Hui to break his vow, all three embraced and had a good laugh.

"The Three Laughers of Tiger Ravine" would become a popular subject for artists and a symbol of the ultimate unity of the "Three Ways" of Confucianism, Buddhism and Taoism. Why has this laugh echoed down through the ages? It speaks of a world in which friendship can overcome differences, in which the things we take seriously can also be viewed with humor and broadmindedness. This attitude, summed up in Lin Yutang's *The Importance of Living*, has always characterized Chinese civilization at its best. Hopefully it will find a place in the civilization that East and West are now engaged in building together.

1 -"weak Chin emperor" - The dynastic name "Chin" is pronounced "Jin," so this only appears to be a terrible pun. The first dynasty to unify all of China, the Ch'in (note the apostrophe after "Ch") is pronounced like the English "chin," and this is the source of our word for China.

2 -"gave up his seal" - Officials had a stamp or seal that served as their signature and badge of office. In the preface to "Returning Home" Tao gives another excuse for quitting, but the two accounts are not incompatible, and the popular story strikes closer to home.

MR. FIVE WILLOWS[3]

We do not know where this gentleman comes from, nor do we know his family or courtesy names. Beside his cottage grew five willow trees, and from these he took his literary name. Leisurely, peaceful, a man of few words, he does not long for honor or profit. He loves to read books, but doesn't care about exact interpretations. When he truly does understand something, he is so happy he forgets to eat.

By nature he is fond of wine, but his family is poor and he doesn't get to enjoy it often. Friends and kinfolk, knowing his situation, sometimes buy wine and invite him over. When he drinks he will empty the jug, with no other purpose than getting drunk. Once drunk, he retires without regret.

The walls around his home are quiet, but scarcely shelter him from wind and sun. His short robe is torn and patched, his rice basket and gourd often empty. And yet he is at peace like this.

He often writes things to amuse himself and somehow explain his ideals. Completely oblivious to gain and loss, he will go on this way to the end.

APPRAISAL:

Ch'ien Lou had a saying: "Not sad about poverty and low position, not anxious for honor and wealth." Perhaps his words apply to a man like this. Drinking wine and making poems to please his heart, is he not like a man of ancient times?[4]

3 - Tao's tongue-in-cheek autobiography is modeled on Pan Ku's Han dynasty biographies, which included a character appraisal at the end. Friends like Yen Yen-chih (see his funeral elegy for Tao on page 93) vouched for the accuracy of this portrait.

4 - "ancient times" - Literally "Lord Wu Huai and Lord Ko T'ien's times," legendary rulers of ancient China.

RETURNING HOME

The Empty Boat

The empty boat drifts free, without an oar
Turn and turn again, without an end
The year begins; look up, and suddenly
We are halfway through the cycle of the stars

At the south window, nothing worn or withered
The north woods lush with leaves and fruit
The Spirit Abyss pours out its timely rain
At dawn's flush, music of the summer winds

Since we have come, must we not also go?
Man's destiny includes a final day
Embracing the endless, we await the end
Bent arm for a pillow, who can harm the peace within?

Accepting the changes, whether smooth or rough
Letting go of desire's ups and downs—
Already living on such lofty heights
What need is there to climb the sacred peaks?

Written while Passing through Ch'u-o
when First Serving as an Aide to the General

In my youth unconcerned with worldly affairs
Carefree, my mind on my lute and books
I was content with a coarse cloth quilt
Though often empty, I was always peaceful

Then I met with a dark and bitter time
Straying with slack reins on the common highway
My orders came; I had to pack by morning
Suddenly parted from my fields and garden

Smaller and smaller, the lonely boat recedes
Endless thoughts of returning wring my heart
Who would not think this journey far,
Climbing, descending more than a thousand li?

My eyes are weary of strange roads and rivers
My heart is longing for my hills and marshes
Gazing at clouds, I am humbled by high-flying birds
Looking at water, I'm shamed
   by the free-swimming fish

From the first, the truth has been planted in my heart
Who says we're confined to shadows and illusions?
For now, I'll follow the changes where they go
And someday return to a humble hermit's cottage

Returning to Fields and Gardens

I.

From youth out of step with the world
By nature loving hills and mountains
Snared by mistake in the dusty net
Suddenly thirty years have passed

The caged bird longs for the forest
The pond fish pines for deeper water
Clearing a field in the southern wilds
I'll stand by my stupidity, go back to farming

My homestead has a little land
A thatched roof to cover a mat
Peaches and plums spread their limbs in front
Willows and elms shade the eves in back

In the hazy distance, haunts of men
Smoke drifting, drifting from the little village
Dogs bark in the deep lanes
Roosters crow from the mulberry trees

Within my doors no worldly dust
Bare rooms furnished with abundant leisure
For so long I was trapped inside a cage
Now I return to my natural self again

II.

Out in the country, men's affairs are few
Wheel and harness rare in the narrow lanes
When the sun is bright I close my brushwood gate
Abandon all dusty thoughts in my empty rooms

Now and then wandering overgrown paths
Parting the grass we come and go
No idle chatter when we chance to meet—
Only how the hemp and mulberry grow

The mulberry and the hemp grow daily taller
Day by day my fields are growing broader
We live in fear that frost and sleet will come
And everything will wither with the weeds

III.

Planting beans beside South Mountain
The grass grows thick, the bean sprouts thin and few
At dawn setting out to tame the wasteland's weeds
Clad in moonlight, hoe on my shoulder, I return

The path is narrow, trees and grasses tall
My clothes are damp with the evening dew
I don't begrudge wet clothes at all
If only my hopes don't come to naught

IV.

Long since I've wandered mountains and marshes
Enjoying the forest and the wilderness
Today I take my children and their cousins
Parting the thickets, we find a deserted village in
the wilds

We linger among the grave mounds
Ponder the dwellings of departed men
Wells and hearths are all that's left
Mulberry and bamboo rotted and decayed

I ask a man who's gathering firewood
"These people—where did everybody go?"
The woodcutter answers me in turn:
"Dead and gone, and nothing left of them."

"In one generation, courts and cities change."
This is certainly not an empty saying
Man's life is like a magical illusion
When finished, it returns to nothingness

V.

Sad and alone, I return with my walking stick
The path twists through rough and rugged underbrush
A mountain stream runs clear and shallow
Here I stop and wash my feet

The filter dripping with fresh wine
I invite the neighbors to share a single chicken
The sun goes down, the house grows dark
A bramble fire serves for candlelight

Joy comes, and we regret the night is short
Already day is dawning once again

Returning Home

Introduction

My family was poor. Plowing and planting did not supply our needs. The house was full of children, the rice jar empty, and I couldn't see how to get by. Friends and relatives urged me to become an official, but even when I agreed, it wasn't easy. Having some business to take care of, I made a good impression on the local lords. Then an uncle, seeing my distress, got me appointed to a little town. With so much unrest abroad I was afraid to serve far away. P'eng-tse was a hundred li from home, but the public fields yielded plenty of rice for wine, so I took the post.

After a few days I wanted to go back home. Why? My spirit needs freedom, and hates to be forced or restricted. Hunger and cold are bitter, but going against my nature makes me sick. When I'm involved in official affairs, I'm just serving my mouth and belly. To abandon my ideals makes me ashamed.

Still, I was going to stick it out for a year, then pack my bags and slip away in the night. But soon my sister, Madam Ch'eng, died at Wu-ch'ang. Wanting to go there as soon as possible, I gave up my post. Midautumn to winter, I had been in office about eighty days when events let me do as I wished.

I have titled this piece "Returning Home." Eleventh month of the year I-ssu (December, 405 A.D.)

Returning Home

Oh, to go back home again
My fields and garden have gone to weeds.
        Why not return?
I have made my soul the servant of my body
Why live with this regret and lonely grief?

No use blaming myself about the past
I know the future still can be redeemed
In truth, I haven't gone so far astray
Yesterday's wrong can be set right today

Far, far the boat sails, urged onward by the wind
My loose robe flaps and flutters in the breeze
I question travelers about the way ahead
Impatient that dawn's light is faint and dim

At last I can see my cottage roof
Filled with joy, I break into a run
The servants come out to welcome me
My little children waiting by the door

The three paths are all overgrown
But the pine trees and chrysanthemums are fine
Taking my children's hands, I go inside
And find the jug is full of wine

I pull up the jug and pour myself a cup
A glance at the courtyard trees lights up my face
I lean out the south window, proud and satisfied
How easy to be content with a modest place....

I stroll the garden every day for pleasure
Although there is a gate, it's always shut
Leaning on a staff, I rest and wander
Sometimes I lift my head, gazing far away

Clouds, without a care, rise from the mountains
Birds, tired of flight, know when to head for home
The light grows dim, the sun begins to set
Stroking the bark of a solitary pine, I linger long

Oh, to go back home again....
Please, no more business, no more aimless drifting
The world and I will forget about each other
Riding a carriage again, what would I seek?

I enjoy fond conversations with my family
The pleasure of lute and books will banish care
The farmers tell me when springtime comes
There's "business" in the western fields out there

Sometimes I call for a covered cart
Sometimes I row a solitary boat
Far and deep I search secluded valleys
By rough and rugged paths I cross the hills

The trees turn joyful and lush with leaves
The springs start to trickle, then begin to flow
It is good the ten thousand things all have their season
I am glad my life's journey has finally come to rest

It is finished!
How long do we dwell in the house of the body?
Why not let the heart choose to go or stay?
Why blunder so blindly and anxiously along the way?

Riches and honor are not what I desire
Nor do I have any hope for Heaven
Content on a lovely morning to go out
Sometimes planting my staff to weed and hoe

Climbing the eastern hills, whistling carelessly
Gazing on a clear stream, writing poems
Just riding out the changes to the end
Content to follow my destiny, without a doubt

Spring at my Farm, Thinking of the Ancients

The ancient master[11] left us a teaching:
"Care for the Way, care not about poverty"

I revered him, but he was beyond my reach
So I turned my mind to this life of toil

Grasping a plough handle, glad for the season's work
Smiling and laughing, I urge on the farmers

The level fields welcome winds from afar
The lovely sprouts hold new life in their hearts

Although the harvest has not yet come
These everyday things still give us great pleasure

Ploughing and planting have their times of rest
No traveler stops to ask about the way

At sunset we're all headed home together
A jug of thick wine will cheer up the neighbors

Singing long, I close my brushwood gate
Somehow, I'm now one of the farmers

Naming My Son

VI.

Grandfather was grave and dignified
"At the beginning, mindful of the end"
In his dealings he was straight and square
Spreading peace and kindness everywhere

My father was a noble soul
Dispassionate, empty, quiet
He walked among the winds and clouds
Indifferent to pleasure as to pain

VII.

Alas that I alone am lacking talent
I look up to them, but cannot touch them
I regard my white temples with shame
Standing alone with my shadow

"Of all the three thousand crimes
The worst is not having an heir"
Truly, I thought of this saying
When I heard your tiny cries

VIII.

This day was divined as fortunate,
This hour a happy one
I give you the name of Yen
And the courtesy name of Ch'iu-ssu

"Morning and evening mild and reverent"
Ponder this saying and abide in it
Always keep Kung Chi in mind
Always aspiring to live like him

IX.

"An ugly man whose child is born at night
Rushes out to fetch a light"
Everyone surely shares these thoughts
Why would I be the only one?

"After having seen him born
You only hope he has ability"
Although it's a common saying
The feelings behind it are real

X.

Oh sun, oh moon!
Soon you will say goodbye to childhood
"Good luck doesn't come without striving
But bad luck is easy to find"

"Early to rise and late to sleep"
A good saying, if you are gifted
For those who are lacking in talent, alas
It's over before you begin!

Reply to Secretary Kuo

I.

Thick trees in front of my house
Store the cool shade in midsummer

The joyful South wind comes in season
Swirling and eddying, opening my gown

I let go of the world, embracing leisure
Resting and rising, enjoying my lute and my books

Garden vegetables I have in plenty
Grain from last year still in store

In governing oneself, one must set limits
More than enough is not what I desire

Pounding the rice, I make a lovely brew
When the wine is ripe I pour myself a little

My young son, playing here beside me
Tries to talk, but cannot yet make words

These things make me happy once again
For now I can forget an official's cap

I gaze up at the white clouds, oh so distant
Remembering the ancients, oh how deep

Harvesting Early Rice in the Western Fields

The aim of life is to find the Way
But the Way begins with food and clothing
How can you not provide for these
And still seek for peace of mind?

Spring begins with the usual tasks
Now, come autumn, we can see the harvest
I get up at dawn to do my humble work
At sunset come home loaded down with grain

The hills are heavy with dew and frost
The air turns cold earlier there
How could the life of a farmer not be hard?
There's no way to avoid the difficulty

But this weariness in all four limbs
Will spare us from other troubles
I wash up and rest beneath the eaves
A cup of wine relaxes my face, my mind

Long, long ago lived Chu and Ni
A thousand years, and yet we share one spirit
I only hope to go on and on like this
I won't complain that my body has to plow

Living in Retirement on the Ninth Day

Preface

Though living a retired life, I still delight in the name of the Double Nine. Autumn chrysanthemums fill my garden, but I have no way to get wine. In vain I sip chrysanthemum tea, and put my feelings into words:

Our years are few and our desires many
So everyone wants a long life

When day and month reach this auspicious date
the common man rejoices in its name

The dew is cold, the summer wind has ceased
The sky is clear, the constellations bright

Swallows have fled without leaving a shadow
Now comes the noisy honking of the geese

Wine can banish a hundred cares
Chrysanthemums keep us from growing old

What can a poet in a thatched hut do
Empty, watching the seasons rolling by?

Empty wine jug shamed by a dusty cup
Cold autumn flowers doomed to bloom in vain

Cinching my robe, I sing, alone and idle
Out of my reverie deepest feelings rise ·

Steadfast retirement holds many joys
Who says that lingering long is doing nothing?

Begging for Food

Hunger came, and I had to go
But where?

I walked until I reached a town
Knocked on a door and said some stumbling words

The master guessed what I was after
He gave me that and so much more

We chatted on from day's end into night
Draining our cups as the wine jug passed around

Joyful in our new-found friendship
We sang the old songs, then composed some new ones

You are as kind as Han's old washerwoman
I am embarrassed that I lack his talents

How can I thank you for these precious gifts?
I must repay you from beyond the grave

The Bitter Cold Year

Bitter cold, the twilight of the year
Clutching my coat, I seek out the sun on the porch

In the south garden, nothing green is growing
In the north woods, branches bare and dry

Tilt the bottle, not one drop remains
Look in the kitchen, not one wisp of smoke

Books and poems lie scattered beside my chair
But the sun is sinking, no time now to read

My retired life is not like the Agony in Ch'en
But bitter words are heaped on this worthless head

Where can my heart find comfort, then?
Rely on the ancients—worthy were those men

Reading The Classic of Mountains and Seas

Early summer, grass and trees are growing
Around my house in carefree disarray
Flocks of birds delight in shelter here
Like them, I'm glad to have someplace to stay

My humble lane is far from the highway's ruts
But old friends' carriages still find me
Planting and sowing done this year
I have time to read my books today

With pleasure I pour the spring wine
Pick the garden greens and mallows
A fine rain comes from the east
And a fair wind follows

I float through the tale of the King of Chou
Drift past the pictures of mountains and seas
Each glance embracing time and space, eternity
If not happy now, when would I ever be?

Meeting with Fire

For a thatched cottage on a narrow lane
I gladly gave up splendid carriages

The seasons turned, the wind turned violent
Woods and house both burned up in a flash

In the whole place not a roof was left
We sheltered under two boats by the gate

Distant, distant, the new autumn sky
High overhead, the moon is almost full

Fruits and vegetables begin to grow again
But the frightened birds have not returned

I stand in darkness, thinking distant thoughts
One glance sweeps across the nine heavens

Since youth embracing lonely rectitude
Forty years have suddenly passed by

The body is at the mercy of time's changes
The spirit's home is quiet solitude

Virtue is by nature firm and constant
Jade stone is not as strong or solid

I look back and admire Tung Hu's time
When surplus grain was left out in the fields

The people patted their bellies without a thought
Rising at dawn, at twilight returning to sleep

Since I am not as fortunate as they
I'll be content with watering my garden

Moving House

I.

For a long time I wanted to live in South Village
Not because an oracle advised me
I heard that plain and simple hearts lived there
With them I would gladly spend mornings
                and evenings

I thought about this for a number of years
At last the day has come. A humble cottage
And a roof of thatch—who needs more room
As long as it covers a bed and a mat?

Often the neighbors will drop by, day or night
We'll chat at leisure about the ancient times
Rare writings we'll admire with delight
And clear up any passages in doubt

II.

In spring and autumn come perfect days
For singing poems and climbing mountains
Passing each others' huts, we'll give a shout
And whoever has some wine will pour it out

When busy farming, each goes home alone
When we have time, we think of one another
Thinking of one another, we throw on coats
And never tire of talking and laughing together

There's nothing better than a life like this
And there's no need to hurry off just now
Yes, food and clothing have to be provided
But we can trust to hard work at the plow

Reply to Adviser P'ang

Preface

I've read the poem you gave me many times—I could not stop even if I wanted to. Since we became neighbors, winter and spring have passed again. Liking each other from the first, we became close friends. There's an old saying, "Frequent meetings make friendships." Ours goes beyond that. But human affairs often go astray, and so we have to speak of separation.

Master Yang wept at the parting of ways, and ours too is no ordinary grief. I have been ill for many years, and have written nothing in all that time. Never gifted, now I am old and sick. But I want to observe the proper custom and give you something to remember when we're parted.

Good friends need not be old acquaintances
A chance encounter may be all it takes
I have a guest who enjoys the things I like
Always admiring my grove and garden

Our conversation is not of common things
We talk about the ancient sages' books
And if there happens to be a jug of wine
We might amuse ourselves with a little drink

I am indeed a retired scholar now
No longer scurrying to east and west
"With things, the new; with men, the old are best"
This feeble brush may still have much to say

Bodies are bound by mountains and streams
Feelings can travel ten thousand li
Please take care of the man I care about
Who knows the year when we shall meet again?

Enjoying Ourselves Under the Cypresses
at the Chou Family Tombs

The weather today is fine
A clear wind in the flute, a singing zither
Touched by those beneath the cypress trees
How could we not find happiness here?

Voices idly spinning out new songs
Green wine relaxing dear, beloved faces
We don't know what tomorrow has in store
More reason then to sing our hearts out now

Poems After Drinking Wine

Preface

I live a retired life with few pleasures, and lately the nights have been getting longer. By chance I happen to have a famous wine, and not a night goes by that I don't drink it. Alone with my shadow, I drain the cup and soon discover that I'm drunk. Once drunk, I write some lines for my amusement. And so these pages piled up, in no particular order. I asked a friend to copy them out, so we could enjoy them and have a good laugh.

Good and Bad Luck

Good and bad luck never linger
Everyone plays and gets played

Old Master Shao in his melon field
Was once lord of all he surveyed

Winter cold takes turns with summer heat
Men too—when one is in, the other's out

The wise man knows and understands
And never suffers any more from doubt

When chance throws a jug of wine his way
He's happy every night to tip its spout

The Way Has Been Lost

The Way has been lost for a thousand years
Folks now keep a tight rein on their feelings

They have wine, but they're afraid to drink it
Always worried about their reputations

Whatever my body might be good for
Isn't it only good for this one life?

And how long does this one span last?
Swift and startling as a lightning flash

Solemn and serious all their hundred years—
Tell me, what do they expect to gain from this?

The Lost Bird

Seeking a place to roost, the bird lost from the flock
The sun is setting, still it flies alone

Hither and thither without a place to rest
As night grows dark its call grows sadder still

Shrill cries longing for a distant light
Frantic, it finds no shelter nor support

At last it alights upon a lonely pine
And folds its wings, its journey at an end

The bitter wind has stripped the other trees
Only the pine's shade and shelter never fails

The bird has found a place to rest its bones
It won't give up this perch for a thousand years

My Cottage

I built my cottage where other men dwell
But the clatter of horse and carriage does not intrude

You ask how such a thing can be
A distant soul surrounds itself with solitude

Picking chrysanthemums under the eastern hedge
Softly, the South Mountain rises into view

The mountain air so beautiful at sunset
Overhead, the homeward flocking birds

Within these things is something real and true
I want to explain it, but I have no words

Autumn Chrysanthemums

Lovely, the colors of autumn chrysanthemums
I pluck the flowers, dripping with the dew

Float them in this sadness-forgetting stuff
And worldly cares grow distant, dim

Alone with the jug, I offer myself a drink
Cup empty, and the jug politely bows

Sun settling down, all nature comes to rest
Returning birds fly singing to the woods

I whistle on the eastern porch, content
Having somehow found my life again

Two Guests

I have two guests who always lodge together
Their likes and dislikes, though, are poles apart

One gentleman loves getting drunk alone
The other spends the whole year sober

Sober and Drunk, they laugh at one another
Neither agrees with one word from the other

Always following the rules—how stupid!
Better to have an independent spirit

A word of advice for the drunken guest—
When the sun is snuffed out, light a candle

Old Friends

Old friends appreciate my inclinations
Lugging a jug along, we go together

Parting the brambles to sit beneath the pine
A cup or two, and everybody's feeling fine

Raucous old graybeards gabbing, garbling words
Losing all order as we pour our drinks

When I have no idea who I am
Who gives a damn what anybody thinks?

Vast, vague, enchanting place to dwell
Deep is the taste of wine....

Wine Stopper

My homestead stops where the town begins
My wandering has stopped and I'm at leisure

Strolling, I stop at my brushwood gate
Beneath a shady tree I stop and sit

For food I can't stop wanting garden greens
To stop and play with kids my greatest treasure

For so long I could not stop drinking wine
When I did stop there was no more pleasure

When I stopped at night I couldn't sleep
Stopping at dawn, I couldn't crawl out of bed

Day after day I firmly resolved to stop
But when I stopped my heart began to flutter

That stopping was a pain, I understood
I couldn't see what stopping had to offer

Then I stopped and thought about the gain
From stopping, and this morning stopped for good

Going forward from this final stop
My next stop is the Isle of the Immortals

Full stop. A pure glow settles on my face
A million years of bliss without a stop!

Body, Shadow, and Spirit

Noble or humble, wise or foolish, everyone strives to preserve their life. This is a great delusion. I have set forth here the grievances of the Body and its Shadow, then made Spirit speak for Nature to resolve them. Gentlemen who are interested in such things will understand my intention.

I. Body says to Shadow

Heaven and Earth are immortal
Mountains and streams untouched by time
Plants and trees obey an eternal law
Wilting with frost and flourishing with dew

Man, they say, has the wisdom of a god
But he alone is unlike all the rest—
Now you see him in this world
Then suddenly he's gone for good

Who notices the absence of one man?
Will even his friends and family sigh for him?
All that remains are his everyday things
To bring a tear of sorrow to the eye

I have no art to soar above these changes
What must be must be, without a doubt
I only hope you'll heed these words—
When offered wine, don't foolishly refuse it

11. Shadow says to Body

We cannot speak of saving our own life
Defending it is a bitter, awkward business
I'd love to roam the peaks of the immortals
But they are distant, and the way is lost

Ever since we first met one another
We've never tasted different joys or griefs
Resting in shade sometimes we're briefly parted
But in the sun we're never separated

This togetherness can't last forever
In utter darkness we'll both be extinguished
The body dies. To think one's name will perish too
Sets the five feelings on fire

Good deeds leave a memory of loving kindness
Why not, then, devote yourself to this?
Wine is good for quenching cares and sorrows
But honest work is certainly not worse

III. The Spirit Explains

The Great Being's power is impartial
Its myriad ways all flourish naturally
How can Man stand between Heaven and Earth
If not for me?

Although you and I are separate things
From birth we've been attached to one another
Firmly joined, we've known great joy together
How could we not speak freely to each other?

The Three Great Emperors were holy men
But where are they?
P'eng-tsu longed for endless years
Despite his desire, he could not make life stay

Old and young die just the same
Wise or stupid, death makes no distinction
Get drunk every day, you'll forget your fate
But won't that only hasten your demise?

Doing good is a constant source of pleasure
Why should anyone need to praise you for it?
But constant brooding harms my life
Better to let things go and follow fate

Float upon the waves of life's great changes
Unperturbed by pleasure or by fear
Accept the end when its proper time draws near
Never again let it trouble your solitude

The Peach Blossom Spring

In the Tai-yuan period of the Chin dynasty, a fisherman of Wu-ling was making his way up a stream, paying no attention to the distance he had traveled. Suddenly he came upon a grove of peach trees in blossom. For hundreds of yards along the stream, nothing but peach trees. The ground was covered with fragrant herbs and strewn with fallen flowers.

The fisherman kept on going to see how far the peach grove went. Finally, at the foot of a mountain, he found the spring from which the stream came gushing forth. Then he saw an opening in the mountain, from which a light appeared. Curious, he left his boat and ventured into the cave, which was very narrow, barely wide enough to squeeze through.

But after a while it opened onto a wide and level plain. Impressive houses stood amidst rich fields and beautiful ponds, with thickets of mulberry trees and bamboo. Dogs barked and cocks crowed to one another. Paths criss-crossed the fields, with men and women going back and forth, planting and working. They were dresses strangely, like foreigners. Old folks and children were playing and having fun.

When they saw the fisherman they were quite surprised, and asked him where he came from. Having answered their questions, he was invited to one of their homes, where they served him wine and killed a chicken for dinner. When the other villagers heard about him, they came to visit.

The people told the fisherman how their ancestors, fleeing troubles in the time of Qin, brought wives and children to this distant place, and never came out again. They had lost all touch with those outside. They asked him what had happened in the world. They had never heard of the Han dynasty, much less of the Wei and Chin. The fisherman told them as best he could, one thing after another. They all sighed with sorrow and wonder.

Others invited him to their houses, regaling him with food and wine. Finally after several days he took his leave. Saying goodbye, the people said, "Please don't mention us to those outside."

Emerging once more, he found his boat. All the way back he carefully noted every place he passed. Reaching the capital of the prefecture, he went to the magistrate and told his story. The magistrate promptly dispatched a man to go with him. They sought out the places he remembered, but got confused and never found the way.

A high-minded scholar, Liu Tzu-chi of Nanyang, heard about it and joyfully made plans to go there. But he fell ill and died before he could leave. After that there was no one who "asked about the ford."

The Peach Blossom Spring

When the First Emperor upset Heaven's order
Worthy men fled from the world
Huang and Ch'i went to Shang Mountain
These people also departed
Little by little their footprints faded,
The paths they fled by overgrown, abandoned

They encourage one another at their farming
When the sun sets, all go home to rest
Mulberry and bamboo give ample shade
Beans and millet planted in their season
Long threads are drawn from silkworms in spring
No king taxes the autumn harvest

Overgrown paths criss-cross the fields
Roosters and dogs crow and bark at one another
The people's customs cling to ancient ways
In their clothing there are no new fashions
Children are free to wander about and sing
Old greybeards get to stroll and visit friends

When plants grow lush they live in peace
When trees are bare they feel the bitter wind
Although they don't have chronicles or calendars

Four seasons somehow still complete the year
Living in harmony, brimming with happiness
Why should they strive to be learned or wise?

Their strange ways hidden for five hundred years
One morning revealed their mysterious world
The pure and the shallow spring from different
       sources
Soon their secret was hidden once again

Gentlemen who stay inside the square,
How can you grasp what's beyond the noise and dust?
I wish to walk lightly on the wind
To soar on high in search of my true friend

Lament in the Ch'u Mode

for Secretary P'ang and Scribe Teng

Dark and distant is the Way of Heaven
Dim and shadowy the ghosts and spirits

Since I bound my hair and thought about my duty
Six times nine my years of strife and struggle

A young man newly capped in times of trouble
As soon as we set up house I lost my wife

Fire burned my cottage to the ground
Insects took their pleasure in my fields

Wind and rain came down from all directions
The harvest hardly enough to feed one mouth

Summer days were long and hungry
Winter nights we slept without a cover

When evening came we longed to hear the cock crow
At dawn we wished the crow would fly away

It's all my doing, why should I blame Heaven
For all the grief and hardship I've encountered?

A name left after death, alas
Means no more to me than a floating spirit

Alone, I am moved to sing a song of sadness
If only a friend knew the music in my heart

Scolding My Sons

White hair now covers my temples
My flesh has the firmness of mush

But though I have five young, strapping sons
Not one cares for paper or brush

A-shu's years now equal eight plus eight
He has no equal when it comes to being lazy

At fifteen, A-shuan should be reading books
But poetry drives him crazy

Even though they're both thirteen
Yung and Tuan can't add six and seven

T'ung-tzu is almost nine years old
Hunting pears and chestnuts is his heaven

Well, if that's the way my fate has added up
Pour me some more of that stuff inside this cup!

To My Sons, Yen and the Others

...I am past the age of fifty. In my youth I knew extreme distress. Because of my family's poverty, I was always hurrying east and west. My nature is inflexible, my talent poor; many things are disagreeable to me. Weighing my situation, I knew I was headed for worldly misfortune. So I withdrew from the world, which meant that your childhood knew cold and hunger. I was moved by the wife of Ju-chung, who consoled her recluse husband. But I grieve that my own wife and neighbors do not understand me. Amid such bitter feelings, I am truly lonely and disconsolate.

In my youth I studied my lute and my books. I loved the quiet. When I unrolled a scroll and understood something, I was so happy I forgot to eat. When I saw trees spreading shade and heard the birds singing I was once more filled with joy. Often in summer, when I lay under a northern window and a cool breeze came, I would think myself a man of ancient times.

My ideas are shallow and my learning scant, but I think these words are worth something. Since becoming ill, I have gradually grown weaker. Friends and relatives have not neglected me, always coming to help with medicine and acupuncture. Yet I fear my allotted time is almost over.

You are all young and our family poor, without servants. How can you escape the work of gathering wood and drawing water? This preys on my mind, but what is there to say? Though you are not all from one mother, you must keep in mind that all within the Four Seas are brothers.

Fan Chih-ch'un was a man of principle of the Chin dynasty. Seven generations of his family shared the same property, but there were no resentful faces. In the *Book of Songs* it is said:

> I look up to high mountains
> The great road I travel

Even if you cannot attain this, strive for it wholeheartedly. Take care of yourselves! What more can I say?

In the Old Days

In the old days, when my elders spoke
I was disgusted, stopping up my ears
Now that I am all of fifty years
I sound a lot like those old-fashioned folk

Seeking the joys of my youth?
I no longer savor those dishes
Faster and faster time whirls, in truth
Regardless of anyone's wishes

Inheritance? Forget it, son
I plan to spend it all on booze and swill
If I don't leave a dime to anyone
I won't have to write up a will

A Substitute for Farming

I'm not looking for a substitute for farming
Fields and mulberries are my chosen work

But though I've never left my work untended
Still, cold and hungry, I live on dregs and husks

I ask for no more than a belly full
Enough rice to get by is all I want

Coarse cloth against the winter chill
Loose linen for the summer heat

If even these are beyond my reach
Then things are sad indeed

Everyone gets what they deserve
Only the simple-minded lose their place

If that's the way it is, then fine
Let me at least enjoy this cup of wine

I Remember the Prime of My Youth

I remember the prime of my youth
Even without music, I was happy
The four seas could not hold back my ambitions
Raising my wings, I dreamed of distant flights

Months and years have slipped away
So has my youthful spirit ebbed
Now when pleasures come they do not cheer me
Ever and ever more worries on my mind

Little by little my vital strength declines
Daily I realize I'm not the same
A boat in the rapids can't stop for a second
Roughly I'm pulled along without a rest

How much longer is the way ahead?
Who knows where I will drop my anchor?
The ancients treasured every inch of shadow
I think about this, and I feel afraid

The Sun and the Moon Cannot Linger

The sun and the moon cannot linger
The four seasons hustle each other along
Frigid wind shakes the bare branches
The long path is piled with fallen leaves

The fabric frays as time keeps turning
Dark black hair turned prematurely white
Once the pale sign is placed upon your brow
The road ahead grows ever narrower

My home is only a traveler's inn
And I a guest who must depart
Away, away—where shall I go?
My ancient home is up there on South Mountain

Burial Songs

I.

If you have life you must also have death
Our impending end is not an unfair fate
Last night I was a man like any other
This morning I'm enrolled among the ghosts

My spirit's breath dispersed—to where?
My withered body consigned to the hollow wood
My dear children, looking for their father, cry
My good friends now touch me and weep

Gain and loss I will never know again
How would I be aware of right or wrong?
A thousand autumns. After ten thousand years
Who will remember honor or disgrace?

My only regret—while I was in this world
I never had my fill of drinking wine

II.

Before, I had no wine to drink
Now they fill deep cups in vain
Spring wine, giving rise to floating froth
When will I taste it again?

Tables of food lie heaped before me
Friends and relatives sobbing at my side
I would speak, but my mouth makes no sound
I would see, but my eyes hold no light

Before, I slept in a lofty hall
Tonight I will lie in a desolate village of weeds
One morning we go out the gate
And never come home again

III.

The wild grass how vast, how vast
The white poplars how lonely, lonely

A bitter frost grips the ninth month
As they see me off to the distant fields

No human houses anywhere
High grave mounds rise up all around

The horses look to heaven and cry out
The wind moans long and desolate

Once they close the door of that dark house
No more morning for a thousand years

No more morning for a thousand years!
Virtue, intelligence, what good are they now?

Those who have come to send me off
All return to their homes

For my family some grief remains
As for the others, they're already singing

Dead and gone. What more is there to say?
Leave my body to be one with the mountainside

Elegy for Myself

The year is Ting-mao (427), the month Wu-i (October). The heavens are cold, the nights long. The atmosphere is solemn, lonely. Wild geese are departing on their journey. Grasses turn yellow, leaves fall. Master Tao is about to leave this traveler's inn and return to his original home. His friends are filled with grief. They will gather for his funeral feast this evening, bringing offerings of food and libations of clear wine. Already their faces are growing dim, their murmurs faint. *Wu hu ai tsai.* I weep and cry Alas!

Vast, vast is creation
Far, far away is high Heaven
Heaven gives birth to the ten thousand things
And so it was my lot to be a man

Ever since I became a man
My fortune has been poverty
My basket and gourd often empty
Thin linen for my winter clothes

Joyfully I brought water from the valley
Went singing as I gathered firewood
Remote and secluded was my brushwood gate
And yet I was busy both day and night

Spring and autumn changing places
Always there was gardening to do
Sometimes weeding, sometimes hoeing
So it thrived and so it grew

Pleasure from plain, simple writing
Harmony from the seven strings
Winters I bathed in the sunlight
Summers I plunged in the spring

Never laboring too long or hard
My heart remained always at leisure
Enjoying the fortune Heaven gave me
So they passed away, my hundred years

Only these hundred years—
How people cling to them, afraid
Of not achieving anything, hoarding
their days, hating to let the seasons go

To be honored in life
And remembered after death...
Ah well, I've gone my solitary way
Always different from the rest

Since I never sought their favor
How could they darken my obscurity?
Unbending, steadfast in my humble cottage
I drank my wine and wrote my poetry

Knowing well our fate, our destiny
Who can be completely free of care?
But now the final change has come
I find I can face it without regret

I've lived a long life
Seeking only solitude
To meet the end in one's old age,
What more can anyone desire?

Heat and cold have passed away
Not to be is not like being
My wife's family comes in the morning
My friends hurry over at night

They bury me out in the wild
Hoping my ghost will lie in peace
Dark, dark is my journey
Lonely, lonely the door into the tomb

Buried not in shameless luxury
Nor yet with bones completely bare
Empty, ah, and quite extinguished now...
My sighs? Already vanished in the air

Raise no grave mound, plant no tree
Sun and moon will pass the time with me
I never cared for fame before my death
What good will it do me after?

Man's life is truly difficult
Why would death be any different?
Wu hu ai tsai! I weep and cry Alas!

Funeral Elegy for the Summoned Scholar Tao

Yen Yen-chih

*Excerpts from the elegy spoken at Tao's funeral
by his dear friend Yen Yen-chih.*

Tao Yuan-ming lived in seclusion among the southern hills. He truly possessed a simple heart. In a crowd he remained solitary. When he spoke, his quiet was all the more apparent. In youth he suffered poverty and illness. When his mother was old and his sons young, he worked diligently to support her and supply their needs. He declined three offers of office before becoming Magistrate of P'eng-tse. But his principles were not in accord with this position, so he gave up his office and followed his true desires.

Thus he freed himself from the troubles of his times and set his mind on things beyond the world. He watered his garden and raised vegetables, wove shoecords and plaited straw mats to pay for grain. His mind delighted in rare writings; his nature found pleasure in wine.

When an imperial order summoned him to serve as Archivist, he pleaded illness and did not take the post. He died aged sixty-three years at Ch'ai-sang village in the year 427. His close friends mourned him; distant scholars felt grief. May he be blessed in the afterlife! Alas for a man pure and true!

A man's deeds are glorified by a funeral elegy; his name is exalted by a posthumous title. If he has been true to virtue and duty, what does his rank matter? This man's generosity and joyfulness, his honesty and self-mastery are in accordance with the rules for posthumous titles. Therefore, having consulted with his friends, it seems fitting to bestow upon him the title of "Summoned Scholar of Tranquil Integrity."

The Elegy

He longed for the ancients and dwelt apart
Concealing his noble lineage
Despising rank and fame
Among those close to him
He considered himself the least
Friendly but capable of dignity
He was learned but never tedious

Master, you followed your heart
And ignored the affairs of the world
Your rank was that of the lowest officer
Your salary equal to the highest farmer's
Then you wrote your poem "Returning Home"
And chose a path of solitary virtue

Once you were free to follow your way
You did nothing against your nature
Drawing water from the mountain streams
You built your home in your family's woods
In morning mist and sunset clouds
Warmth of spring and autumn dark
You opened books, untied your scrolls
Set out wine and strung the lute

In living you were always careful, frugal
Your body suffered poverty and sickness
Others would have refused this hardship
You accepted it as your destiny

The stream is full of turns and twists
Reward is always unpredictable
Who says "Heaven favors the good"?
Truly, it is doubted by the wise

When you had reached middle age
You fell ill with malarial fever
Looking on death as returning home
Regarding misfortune as fortune
You refused to taste of medicine
Refused to look for help in prayer
Facing the dark, you spoke about your death
Keeping your calm and harmony to the end

Wu hu ai tsai! I weep and cry Alas!

With respect I record your tranquil integrity
And try to honor your last requests
Alive, you did not look for wealth

In death you did not ask for aid:
A brief announcement, no money offerings
Little mourning, simple laying out
Where there is dirt, dig a grave
Do not delay in burying the coffin

Wu hu ai tsai! I weep and cry Alas!

We lived as neighbors in the village
Having neither boats nor carriages
Wandering by night, resting by day
I remember how we used to drink together

Once, raising my cup, I quipped:
"A lone upright man is in danger
The perfect square will get its corners chipped
The wise man knows how to bend and relax
As ancient writings tell us to
Take me for your example, do as I do"

You were deeply troubled, and cried out:
"Opposing the crowd invites blame
Whatever withstands the wind is first to fall
If character and talent are not real

97

Honor will not be lasting, nor will fame"

Your voice has grown far off and dim
Who can correct my failings now?
Even the good come to an end
Even the wise must die

Wu hu ai tsai! Alas! Alas! I weep and cry

The Translator

Dan Veach is the founding editor of *Atlanta Review*. His widely-published translations from Chinese, Spanish, Arabic, and Anglo-Saxon have won the Willis Barnstone Translation Prize and the Independent Publisher Book Award. Translations include *Flowers of Flame: Unheard Voices of Iraq* (Michigan State University Press, 2008), *Beowulf & Beyond* (Lockwood Press, 2021), *Songs of The Cid* (Stockcero, 2022), and *Federico García Lorca: Gypsy Romances & Poem of the Deep Song* (Stockcero, 2022). His own poetry can be found in *Elephant Water* (Finishing Line Press, 2012) and *Lunchboxes* (Iris Press, 2019).

The Poet

Tao Yuan-ming, who lived around 400 A.D., stands first in the line of China's great lyric poets. Creator of an intimate, honest, plain-spoken style, Tao was a man whose life spoke as eloquently as his art. Unable to reconcile himself to the corruption and bureaucracy around him, Tao resigned his post as Magistrate to live the humble and difficult life of a farmer. Though his family would have to endure hardship and hunger, the result was some of the greatest poetry in Chinese history. The famous poets of the Tang and Sung, Li Bai, Du Fu, Wang Wei, and Su Dong-po, looked back to Tao as a beloved grandfather, who taught China's poets a new way of living and seeing.

Notes on the Poems

Page 23: "sacred peaks" - Literally "Hua or Sung," two of China's five sacred mountains, which thousands of pilgrims still climb each year.

Pages 24-25: "li" - About a third of a mile. "A thousand li" is the common phrase for a great distance.

"hermit's cottage": Literally "Master Pan's cottage," home of a famous recluse.

Page 26: "dusty net" - This would become a common term for the entanglements of office, and "dust" a byword for worldly concerns.

"dogs...roosters": Reminiscent of "Peach Blossom Spring," Tao's evocation of ancient rural simplicity.

Page 34: "the three paths" - Perhaps a reference to the three spiritual paths of ancient China: Confucianism, Taoism, and Buddhism.

Page 37: "ancient master Confucius." In this passage of the Analects (Lun-yu), he advises gentlemen to serve in government rather than live by farming. Tao felt guilty about not following Confucius' teaching, and many of his poems deal with this conflict.

"ask about the way" - Literally "ask about the ford." Confucius sent his disciple Tzu-lu to ask some recluse farmers the way to the ford. When they advise him to stop trying to change the world and simply withdraw from it, Tzu-lu is reduced to stunned silence. Score one for the farmers!

Page 38: "winds and clouds" - The distractions and distresses of office. Unlike Tao, his father remained calm in the midst of business.

"I look up to them" - As he said about Confucius in the previous poem, he says of his very Confucian forebears.

Page 39: "Yen...Ch'iu-ssu": The names mean "serious" and "thoughtful." Yen is his first son, nicknamed "A-shu" in "Scolding My Sons."

"Kung Chi" was the grandson of Confucius. Tao wanted his son to be a studious little Confucian. "Scolding My Sons" tells us how well this plan worked out.

"rushes out to get a light"" to see if the baby looks like

him. Tao also hopes the son will not be like the father.

Page 40: "Early to rise" -The Chinese proverb is even more demanding than Benjamin Franklin's.

Page 42: "official's cap" - Literally the "flowery hair-pin" which held an official's cap in place.

Page 43: "Chu and Ni" - Recluse farmers from the time of Confucius. They advised his student Tzu-lu to renounce the world altogether.

Page 44: "Double Nine" - The festival of the ninth day of the ninth month. To make a life-prolonging elixir on this day, wine would be infused with chrysanthemum blossoms. With no wine, Tao had to settle for chrysanthemum tea.

The dynastic histories record that on one Double Nine holiday, when Tao had no wine, Governor Wang Hung brought some and they both got drunk. So perhaps this occasion had a happy ending.

Page 45: "lingering long" - Tao is objecting to a line in *Ch'u-tz'u*: "Yet he has lingered long and done nothing."

Page 46: "Han's old washerwoman" - She fed Han Hsien when he was poor and hungry in his youth. After becoming a great lord and general of the Han dynasty, he rewarded her generously.

Page 47: "Agony in Ch'en" - A time when Confucius and his disciples were starving. Tzu-lu asked his master resentfully, "Must a gentleman also endure hardship?" "Yes," replied Confucius, "but a gentleman shows firmness in adversity."

"bitter words" - It may have been family or "Job's friends" urging him to give up farming and seek office. He finds comfort in the ancient master's "firmness in adversity," which would become the watchword of his life.

Page 48: *The Classic of Mountains and Seas* was an illustrated book of strange creatures and places. The tale of the King of Chou comes from a similar book, *Travels of the Emperor Mu*. It's good to see Tao in a brighter mood. If he doesn't deserve happiness, who does?

"highway's ruts" - Signs of worldly business and official occupation.

Page 49: "roofs" - Chinese homes typically had several units surrounding a central courtyard.

Page 50: "Tung Hu's time" was a golden age when everyone had plenty and lived in innocent simplicity.

"watering my garden" - Reminiscent of the ending of *Candide*: "We must cultivate our garden."

Page 51: "passages in doubt" - "Mr. Five Willows" doesn't worry about dubious passages when reading alone, but here he looks forward to thrashing them out with friends. Clearly the "plain and simple hearts" he longs for are retired scholars like himself, with pure hearts but subtle minds. As the next poem shows, he did find at least one such friend.

Page 53: "chance encounter" - Literally "lowered canopy." When Confucius met Ch'eng Pen-tzu by chance, they took down the canopies of their carriages and talked all day.

Page 56: "Master Shao" - Shao P'ing, after the fall of the Ch'in dynasty, was reduced from a Marquis to a melon farmer.

The poems in this series are untitled. Since some of

Tao's best poems are here, titles are supplied for identification.

Page 59: Tao's identification with the bird seeking shelter reminds us of the first verse of "Reading *The Classic of Mountains and Seas*."

Page 61: "chrysanthemums" - Tao's love of chrysanthemums is legendary; the two are inseparable in the Chinese mind.

Page 64: In this tongue-in-cheek tour de force, the character *chíh* (stop) appears in every line. As in English, it has several different meanings in Chinese. Though not formally part of Tao's "Twenty Poems After Drinking Wine," this one is an appropriate "stopper" to the collection.

Page 68: "the five feelings" - Pleasure, anger, sorrow, joy, and resentment. Elsewhere Tao claims not to care for fame, but his Shadow admits to a deep concern for his posthumous reputation.

Page 69: P'eng-tsu was the Chinese Methuselah, who lived 800 years.

Page 71: "the time of Qin" - The First Emperor of the

Qin (or Ch'in) dynasty used brutal force to unite all of China. The Chin dynasty mentioned in the first line was during Tao's own time.

Page 72: "asked about the ford" - A disciple of Confucius asked two recluse farmers the way to the ford. They advised him to give up seeking political reform, like Confucius, and withdraw altogether from the world.

Page 73: Huang and Ch'i were famous recluses.

Page 74: "inside the square" - As in English, a "square" person can be honest and upright and/or narrow-minded and bound by convention. In *Chuang-tzu,* Confucius says that he "wanders inside the square" whereas the recluses and hermits "wander outside the square." In his boldest declaration of independence, Tao bids farewell to the "square" Confucians and sets out on his own path.

Page 75: "Ch'u mode" is a Chinese musical scale.

"bound my hair" refers to a ceremony at the age of puberty.

"a young man capped": The capping ceremony took

place at age twenty.

"the crow": The sun, where a three-footed crow was supposed to live. In other words, they longed for sunset.

Page 76: "a friend" - Literally "a man like Ching-ch'u," who always understood what his friend Po-yu was thinking when Po played the lute. When Ching-ch'u died, Po-yu smashed his lute and never played again.

Page 77: A-shu is his first son, Yen, who also appears in "Naming My Son" and "To My Sons, Yen and the Others." The names in this poem are childhood nicknames or "milk names." His other sons' real names are Ssu, Pin, I, and T'ung.

This poem was considered by some critics to be "unworthy of a sage." Perhaps the critics have forgotten that even "sages" are human. Although Tao's frustration is no doubt real, the tone of affectionate joking is obvious. In a subsequent poem, "In the Old Days," Tao admits he was not always a perfect child either.

Page 78: "I forgot to eat" is similar to the account in "Mr. Five Willows."

Page 79: "not all from one mother" - We don't know

if he had a son by his first wife. If not, the age differences would make it likely that the youngest son Tung (see "Scolding my Sons") was by a third wife or concubine.

"all within the Four Seas are brothers" is a famous saying from the *Lun-yu* (*Analects of Confucius*).

Fan Chih-ch'un was a member of a noted family of scholars who also refused to take office.

"I look up to high mountains": The great historian Ssu-ma Ch'ien had applied this couplet to Confucius, and followed it with a remark similar to Tao's: "Although I cannot reach it, yet my heart inclines toward it."

Page 81: "a substitute for farming "- An official position. The lowest official's salary was a substitute for the amount he would make by farming.

Page 82: "boat in the rapids" - Literally "boat in a valley," from *Chuang-tzu*: "You may hide your boat in a valley...but some dark night a strong man will come and steal it."

"inch of shadow" - An "inch of time" as measured by

the sundial.

Page 83: "sun and moon" - The Chinese characters can also mean "days and months."

"ancient home" refers to his tomb.

Page 84: "Burial songs" are "bearer's songs," to be sung by pallbearers pulling the bier. Though the earliest songs (see below) were actually sung at funerals, the form was adapted for more philosophical musings on death.

Page 85: "lofty hall, village of weeds" - Tao is quoting from other famous burial songs. (Clearly he did not sleep in a "lofty hall" himself.) During the Han dynasty, "Dew on the Garlic" was sung for the funerals of nobility, "Village of Weeds" for officers and commoners.

> *Dew on the Garlic*
>
> On the garlic, the morning dew
> burns away so quickly in the sun.
> The dew disappears
> and tomorrow falls again.
> Once a man is dead and gone

when will he ever return?

Village of Weeds

Who dwells in the village of weeds?
The ghosts gather here,
both the wise and ignorant.
The Lord of Ghosts,
how he hurries us along!
Man's fate won't allow him to linger.

Page 88: "Elegy for Myself" - Although the elegy was
a well-established form by Tao's time, he was the first
to write one for himself. Rising above the pains of age
and poverty, here he presents a balanced assessment
of his life, both its joys and struggles. Probably written
close to his death at age 63, his elegy has, somewhat
eerily, exactly 63 lines.

Wu hu ai tsai (I weep and cry Alas!) - This traditional
cry of grief was first used by the Duke of Ai in his
elegy for Confucius.

Page 89: "hundred years" is a traditional expression
for the human life span.

Page 91: "shameless luxury...bones completely bare" -

The original lines refer to a Sung minister whose elaborate stone coffin took years to carve, and a man named Wang-sun who asked to be buried naked. As we see in his official elegy, Tao requested a modest burial between these two extremes.

"I never cared for fame" - Fame has been called the last temptation of a great soul. Though he struggles with it in "Body, Shadow, and Spirit," here, at the end of his poem and his life, he dismisses it once and for all. We are reminded of Keats' epitaph, "Here lies one whose name was writ on water." Ironically, Tao would become one of China's most famous and beloved poets.

Page 95: "truly, it is doubted by the wise" - This rather shocking sentiment is not uncommon in Chinese elegies. Clearly, a good Confucian could admonish not only the emperor, but even Heaven itself for its failings!

Page 96: "you spoke about your death" is perhaps a reference to "Elegy for Myself."

Page 97: "ancient writings" - *Tao Te Ching*, the ancient Taoist text, advocates flexibility and acceptance of fate.

"take me for your example" - That is, be flexible and willing to serve in office. In contrast, Confucius states that, "A good man may be broken, but cannot be bent."

Companions for the Journey Series

Inspirational work by well-known writers in a small-book format
designed to be carried along on your journey through life.

Volume 29
Taken to Heart: 70 Poems from the Chinese
Translated by Gary Young and Yanwen Xu
978-1-945680-58-8.   104 pages

Volume 28
Dreaming of Fallen Blossoms
Tune Poems of Su Dong-Po
Translated by Yun Wang
978-1-945680-27-4   243 pages

Volume 27
Precious Mirror
Kobun Otogawa
Translated by Gary Young
978-1-945680-21-1   100 pages

Volume 26
Unexpected Development
Klaus Merz
Translated by Marc Vincenz
978-1-945680-14-4   142 pages

Volume 25
A House by Itself
Selected Haiku: Masaoka Shiki
Translated by John Brandi & Noriko Kawasaki Martinez
ISBN 978-1-945680-09-0.   102 pages

Volume 6
A Zen Forest: Zen Sayings
Translated by Soioku Shigematsu
Preface by Gary Snyder
1-893996-30-1   120 pages

Volume 5
Back Roads to Far Towns
Basho's Travel Journal
Translated by Cid Corman
1-893996-31-X   94 pages

Volume 4
Heaven My Blanket, Earth My Pillow
Poems from Sung Dynasty China by Yang Wan-Li
Translated by Jonathan Chaves
1-893996-29-8   288 pages

Volume 3
10,000 Dawns: The Love Poems of Claire and Yvan Goll
Translated by Thomas Rain Crowe and Nan Watkins
1-893996-27-1   88 pages

Volume 2
There Is No Road: Proverbs by Antonio Machado
Translated by Mary G. Berg and Dennis Maloney
1-893996-66-2   118 pages

Volume 1
Wild Ways: Zen Poems of Ikkyu
Translated by John Stevens
1-893996-65-4   152 pages